Invest

How To Make Passive Income From Real Estate Without
Having To Own Or Manage Physical Property

(Why It's A Good Idea And How To Start)

Antonia Mendoza

TABLE OF CONTENT

History And Operations Of The Stock Market............. 1

How Do Dividend Stocks Work?.....................................31

What Carry Out New Investors?...................................52

Underlying Life Principles According To Warren Buffett..71

Simplest Investments For Novices 119

A Successful Penny Stock Trader's Psychology....131

History And Operations Of The Stock Market

Most businesses sell shares to raise money and increase their revenue. The general public can always purchase stocks, and the faster a firm grows, the more expensive its shares become. The majority of traders choose stocks with strong price growth potential. Additionally, they make investments in stocks with strong dividend yields. A trader will try to sell off his shares of a particular stock once he learns that the price is set to drop in order to prevent a loss. Stock trading is the act of buying and selling stocks on a stock exchange.

The stock market depends heavily on stockbrokers. On behalf of investors, they purchase and sell shares as well as provide advice to these clients. Although trading through brokers is simple, the commissions could be a bit pricey, especially for new traders who aren't making much money. However, doing the transaction alone calls for a lot of investigation and analysis. Before you can trade successfully, you must have a solid understanding of the stock market. You must comprehend market trends as well as any variables that may have an impact on them. There is more to making money on the stock market than just buying and selling. You need to understand how specific stock categories are doing on the market and whether prices are subject to change.

Those who still want to play it safe on the market typically deal in shares whose price trends are predictable and steady. For instance, due to their generally more stable pricing, shares offered by manufacturing companies and oil corporations are always safe. Some stocks also pay out respectable dividends. These are advantageous since you can still make money from them even if share prices stay the same.

The market typically consists of both physical places and computer networks and programs.

Common Stock Market Terminology

You need to have some comprehension of the fundamentals involved in this type of trade in order to comprehend the stock market and stock trading. If you wish to succeed in this type of investment, you must learn the terminologies used in the stock market. Trading in the stock market involves using a number of phrases. Here are a few of the most typical.

A trader who buys more shares of a stock whose price is falling is said to be averaging down. As a result, the stock's average purchase price declines. When traders think that the stock price will increase later, they buy at this point.

Blue-chip stocks are those that are listed by well-known businesses or sectors. These companies are typically bought by investors because they offer respectable dividends and earnings.

Bull markets: In a bullish stock market, prices rise steadily over an extended period of time. The bear market, in which prices drop steadily over a lengthy period of time, is the antithesis of this market.

Broker: For a charge, a broker will buy or sell stock shares on behalf of a client.

A person's bid is the amount of money they are prepared to offer in exchange for one share of stock.

A portion of an institution's profits that is distributed to its shareholders is referred to as a dividend. Individuals who own any amount of shares from a certain corporation are called shareholders. Dividends are paid to shareholders by some corporations while they are not by others.

The stock exchange is the location where various stocks are traded. The NYSE and NASDAQ, both of which are located in the United States, are two examples of stock exchanges.

Stock high: A stock high is a condition in which the stock price reaches a higher level than it did previously. Low, which designates the lowest price point of a specific index or stock, is the reverse of this.

Stock margin accounts allow traders and investors to borrow money from brokers to purchase stocks. The term "margin" refers to the discrepancy between the loan's value and the cost of the stock purchased.

Stock portfolio: The collection of stock investments that make up a trader's portfolio. A limitless number of equities may be purchased on the stock market by each investor.

Share market: A market where investors can purchase and sell shares. One excellent illustration of a share market is the stock market.

Each stock has a unique symbol that serves as its representation. This may consist of one to four alphabetic letters.

Stock volatility is the variation in price of a specific stock. The reason why most traders prefer highly volatile shares to those with low volatility is because they can benefit handsomely from the sharp price swings.

Being familiar with these words can help you develop into a skilled trader. Knowing them all will undoubtedly take some time, but once you do, you'll be able to use them in your deals with no trouble. Making good investments in stock market trading requires a thorough comprehension of these terminology.

Role of the Market to Investors and Companies

Investing in the stock market is one of the ways to make a profit. Companies join the market with one aim, to raise more capital for their businesses. They do this to also generate more profits by targeting investors that can help build the business. When it comes to stock trading, companies only offer a portion of its shares to the public, and this is what investors trade-in.

Investors, on the other hand, use the stock market as a medium of completing buy and sell transactions. This is mostly done in real-time and at a profit.

History of the Stock Market

The stock market history has been disagreed upon by several historians. It is somewhat difficult, therefore to state the exact date and time that the stock market was established. One theory coined by Fernand Braudel, a historian, states that Jewish and Muslim merchants were the first people to start stock trading in the 11th century. It is, however, not clear whether this is what led to the present-day stock markets.

Another more reliable theory states that trading began when people engaged in exchanging commodities with each other. This was always carried out in a central place. When money was introduced as a form of exchange, people started engaging in the buying and selling of goods and services.

The stock market began when such trading moved from individual to a country level. As countries traded with each other, several merchants started engaging in large businesses that required big amounts of capital. By then, a single merchant found it impossible and couldn't raise such large sums of money, and it is due to this that investors started trading in groups. Each of the traders contributed a certain amount of capital towards the business. This brought about the concept of joint-stock companies that initially were used by the Dutch traders in 1602.

With time, this idea spread into other countries. Eventually, it became a globally embraced form of trading. As the number of individual shares increased, there arose a need for a central place where investors would exchange them. Stock traders then decided to meet at the London coffeehouse and used it as a central marketplace. They later converted the coffeehouse into what they called the stock exchange. This is how the London Stock Exchange, which is the first exchange ever came about. A similar exchange was established in 1790 in Philadelphia, and in 1792, the market on Wall Street was founded. This slowly continued in various countries, and continents until today. Up to now, several stock exchanges have been established globally. Each exchange offers the cash required to grow the stock trading industry.

The origin of the stock market has also been linked to the colonial government, which sold notes to promote war strategies. These were to be paid back with some interest. During this time, some private banks embraced this as a method to grow their capitals. They, therefore, began to trade in stocks and shares, thus opening a whole new market where people could invest their money. At first, this was only available to the rich, but with time, even the average people were involved.

A meeting between 24 merchants in 1792 contributed to the establishment of the modern New York Stock Exchange. There was rapid growth in the United States during the 80s as more investors bought ownership in some of the famous companies. This made companies expand quickly. During this time, many people started reselling shares at a profit. As time went by, even the small companies started listing their shares on the stock market, which grew to become the American stock exchange. This was later bought in 1998 by NASDAQ which was established in 1971.

As the markets grew, the merchants came up with a regulation that would protect investors from losing their money. However, this did not take place until 1934, after the 1929 stock market crash. This was one of the most fatal crashes in the stock market. The margin rates increased significantly leading to a market decline that caused the Great Depression. Over the years, this market has grown to high levels where billions of shares are traded every day.

Several other crashes have also occurred in the history of stock market trading. These were caused by economic factors as well as traders panic. Some of the notable crashes include:

The Kipper and Wipper, which is one of the oldest. It occurred as a result of the fraudulent cheapening of foreign currencies by traders from the Roman Empire. This occurred between 1621 and 1693

The 1792 panic was a financial deadlock that resulted from credit expansions made by a new bank in the United States

The 1893 panic which was more severe since it caused an immense economic imbalance. There was a sudden decrease in stock prices that led to the closing down of 500 banks

The Japanese asset bubble took place from 1981 to 1986. This resulted in highly inflated stock and real estate costs. This also caused a 10-year crash in Japan's economy, often referred to as the Lost Decade

2007 – 2008 financial crisis. This was a global crisis that was considered worse than any other crash, except the 1939 great depression. The crisis began in the United States and slowly grew into a worldwide crisis.

One thing that was missing in the first stock markets ever invented was stock. The markets resembled the modern stock markets but did not involve the exchange of company shares. Instead, these markets engaged in individual, business, and government debts. The systems used to issue these debts is similar to what is used in stock trading, although the items of trade differed.

The first-ever company to be publicly traded was the East India Company. This is because it was risky to travel to the

East Indies, yet the region had lots of opportunities to explore. Traders who sailed to the region rarely made it home. Some lost their fortunes as well as their lives. Financiers within the area thus had to come up with ways through which they could trade with people from other regions without facing this risk.

Years back, traders had to engage with brokers over the phone whenever they needed to place a stock order. However, with the advancements experienced in technology, most traders can now join with brokers online as soon as they set up their accounts.

The stock market has undergone various changes since its inception. One such change is the technology bubble that took place in the 1990s. During this time, all the stocks that were related to technology experienced a tremendous increase in price. This was followed by a correction period where the prices dropped down to normal again.

This history makes it clear how the stock market dictates price mechanisms. Once in a while, the market gives the buyers a certain kind of "fever" where the prices go higher than the expected normal rate. At other times, traders are filled with uncertainty and fear, and this results in sudden price declines. This perspective is what helps traders to avoid loss during extreme conditions. It also enables them to take advantage of certain opportunities to make more profit from their investments.

Just like any other financial platforms, the stock market has experienced its ups and downs since its inception. From sudden crashes to global slowdowns, the traders have to remain patient during such times if they wish to make something out of it. Today, these markets play a vital role in the economic growth of most countries around the world.

Modern Stock Markets

In the modern world, nearly every country has a stock trading market. Most of these markets came up between the 19th and 20th centuries. This was after the NYSE and LSE exchanges were created. Some world economic powers boast of some of the best and most active stock markets. Each day, traders exchange trillions of dollars on these stock markets.

Several thousand years later, the stock market keeps improving each day. Similar to the early days, traders still meet at a central place to buy and sell their stocks. This is known as the stock exchange. There are several hundreds of physical stock exchanges in the world—some of these work 24 hours each day.

How the Stock Market Works

The stock market is often likened to an auction. Investors engage in the buying and selling of stock shares, and the process involves some form of negotiation. Shares are small percentages of a company's ownership.

The price of a company's shares is often used to determine the number of returns that the company is capable of earning in the future.

During a trade, investors who think the prices of a particular stock will rise to tend to bid on the price going up and those who think the opposite will happen bid on a price decrease. For each share trader, the investor tries to make as much profit as possible. Buyers, on the other hand, strive to get the shares at the lowest price possible so that they can sell these later, at a profit.

People with limited knowledge and experience in the stock market tend to fear to invest in the trade because they are scared of losing their capital. The truth is, the stock market involves some level of risk. However, if the trader is disciplined enough in terms of research and trading, the losses incurred will be minimal. The stock market is by far, one of the trading methods that investors use to build their net worth within a short period.

The stock market operates via several exchanges. The company selling shares lists them on the exchange via IPO or initial public offering. IPO can be defined as the process through which private companies list their shares to the public. This allows the company to make money as public investors purchase its shares. The method also helps companies to transition from private ownership to public ownership. It also assists them in making income from outside investments. For a company to raise an IPO, it has to work with an underwriter. Underwriters help list the shares on stock exchanges. They also assist the investor in determining which exchange to use when trading shares publicly.

The IPO process has been used in the stock market industry for several decades. Once a company lists its shares, investors buy the shares, and the money realized is used by the company to grow its business. Besides purchasing shares from the company, investors can also trade the shares between themselves, depending on the level of supply and demand of the shares.

One factor that determines prices on the stock market is the supply and demand of a particular stock. In this case, supply and demand refer to the level of prices, which the participants on the market are willing to purchase and sell the underlying stock. These levels are derived using computer algorithms.

A trade transaction begins with the buyer offering a bid price for the shares. This amount is always lower than the selling price and the difference between the bid price, and the price that the seller is asking for is called the bid-ask spread. The buyer and seller then negotiate through these two prices until they arrive at a level of agreement.

Brokers

Traders can also buy shares through brokerage accounts or individual retirement accounts. These are opened via an online broker who acts as the middle-person or go-between the trader and the stock exchange platforms.

If you are a beginner, there are two types of brokers that you can engage in for assistance in stock market trading. These are full-service brokers and online or discount brokers.

Full-service brokers are traditional brokers who seek to understand you personally as you engage them. They help assess your financial status as they try to assist you to come up with a long-term financial and trading plan. These assist you make investment decisions by offering you sound financial advice, thus the term full-service. If allowed, such brokers can help meet and manage your financial needs, with the long-term in mind. Since they offer you a number of services, their commissions are often higher than discount brokers. Most beginners need full-service brokers because they are yet to gain experience in the trade.

Discount brokers rarely provide investment advice. They only take stock orders from you and process them to the best of their ability. Since their services are limited, they charge less and do not engage with you on a personal level. The cost of hiring such brokers is always per transaction. Since they do not give you any market tips, you will need to work hard to obtain these from other sources. Besides taking orders, the only other thing that online or discount brokers assist you with is resolving technical issues. A discount broker is only suitable for you if you are well equipped to manage your own investments.

Whether to go for a full-service or discount broker depends on your personal needs. Full-service brokers may be ideal for you if you are willing to pay hefty premiums, but discount brokers are for those with limited finances or those who wish to take the risk of managing their capital by themselves.

Some companies may allow you to purchase shares directly from them. These are often blue-chip organizations that utilize a process known as DSPP or the direct stock purchase plan to allow small traders or investors to gain ownership of the company without going through a stockbroker. The DSPP differs for each organization, and investors must seek to understand this before engaging in any direct stock trades.

Mutual Funds

The stock market carries both risks and rewards. The number of stock items you trade in becomes your stock portfolio. To manage risks, most traders diversify their portfolio to include a wide variety of stocks with different potentials for profits. Such traders do invest in exchange-traded or mutual funds which allow them to trade in several stocks at the same time.

Whether you need to invest in individual stocks or mutual funds is determined by several factors. You must first define the amount of risk that you are able to tolerate and the time you have to research on your financial investments. This is because investing in mutual funds requires that you spend a lot of time researching on the underlying stocks. Another factor is the number of fees and expenses that you are capable of enduring. This also includes the taxes involved in the entire trading process. With mutual funds, you do not purchase a stock but instead, buy some shares for various stocks in the form of a mutual fund.

The stock market utilizes indices to dispatch market conditions and trends to investors. These indices track important details of trading companies and provide this information to the public. Each stock exchange has at least one index that reports its status.

Types of Stocks

The stock market is a massive industry and involves several items. As a beginner, before thinking of investing in the industry, you must understand the various types of stocks available on the market. This will help you determine the kind of stocks you need to trade for you to realize your financial investment goals. There are several types of stocks, and these are often categorized into three classes, namely: large-cap, middle cap, and small-cap stocks.

Large-cap stocks are stocks listed by the largest companies in the world. These are valued at more than $10 billion and form the basis of the stock market. Most investors go for large-cap stocks because they offer higher returns and provide a steadier cash flow. Some examples of such companies include General Electric and Microsoft. Large-cap stocks are owned by several investors from all over the world. They are the safest to trade because they offer more stability in terms of income and investment opportunities. The prices of such companies do not grow as fast as smaller companies, but the investment is worth trying. The companies also pay regular dividends, providing an income to the investors. Since the stock is very liquid, it is easy for traders to exit a position at any point of business without the fear of losing their capital.

Middle cap—or mid-cap stocks—on the other hand, refer to shares of companies whose market capitalization falls between $1 billion and $5 billion. Companies whose stock falls in this category show high potential for growth. These stocks are more popular since they combine the benefits of large-cap and small-cap stocks. They offer great room for investment expansion and are less risky in case of economic downturns.

Small-cap stocks are riskier than the first two. They are from companies whose market valuation is less than a billion dollars. Since the companies are small, it is easy to lose your investment should you decide to trade in such stocks. Such stocks are characterized by small profits and irregular cash flows. Since few people own them, these companies are highly volatile, thus very unstable.

Besides these categories, stocks can be further classified into several different types. Here are some of them.

Common Stock

Common stock refers to a type of stock that is popular among most traders. As you purchase common stock, you are buying shares as well as voting rights from the company. One advantage of common stock is that it generates very high returns over a period of time. This, however, involves a lot of risks. The risk is often at a maximum when the company becomes bankrupt. When this happens, the stakeholders are usually the last people to receive their money back. If the company continues to grow and makes more profit, investors tend to enjoy the best dividends basing on the number of shares held in the company. The voting privilege is also an advantage since for each share that an investor owns, he or she is entitled to elect people who sit on the company board. However, some common stocks do not come with these privileges.

Preferred Stock

This type of stock offers smaller profits. The risk involved in trading preferred stocks is always small since the investor is assured of a fixed amount of returns in the form of dividends. In the event that a company goes bankrupt, stockholders of preferred stock are considered for payment first before paying common stockholders. One disadvantage of preferred stock is that the company can repurchase it without prior notice. Another disadvantage is that preferred stock does not come with voting rights that are present in common stocks.

Growth Stock

Growth stock is stock belonging to a company whose expected return on equity is at least 15 percent. The return on equity is obtained by dividing the net income by the total equity. Companies that list growth stock on the stock market have the potential to grow quickly over a period of time. This gives the stocks a high demand. Usually, there is very little or no dividends earned from this kind of stock, and great returns are only realized in the long term.

Income Stock

This is stock from stable companies. Such companies do not reinvest in their profits. Instead, the profits are shared amongst the investors as a dividend. If you would wish to earn a dividend from your investment, then you can consider buying income stocks. The dividends can be more or less each year, depending on the profits realized by the company. Income stock is more advantageous because it generates more profits than other forms of stocks. It has less volatility as well. One drawback of this kind of stock is that it has limited opportunities in terms of future growth. Such stocks are mostly found in the real estate, utilities, and energy industries as well as in some financial institutions.

IPO Stock

The initial stock that a firm lists for public trading is called an IPO. Since such equities are transient, they might not be accessible in the long run. If you want to invest for the short term, you can trade in these companies.

Dollar Stock

On the stock market, penny stocks are available for less than $5. These equities are regarded as high-risk due to the fact that they are held by faltering businesses. The majority of penny stocks do not trade more quickly, despite occasionally being heavily bought.

In various nations, penny stocks may be defined differently. For instance, penny stocks are those that trade for less than $1 on the stock market in the United Kingdom. These stocks are typically avoided by professional investors due to their higher volatility and decreased liquidity. They are more vulnerable to deception as well.

Worth Stock

Value stocks are shares whose value has increased. The low pricing of this stock present a significant opportunity for profit. Value stocks are more reliant on a company's performance and earnings prospects. Value stocks are bought by investors in the anticipation that the price will increase and they will profit from it. Value companies often have low price to book ratios, low price to earnings ratios, and high dividend yields.

Speculative Stock This form of stock frequently entails huge risks and extraordinarily big profits. Instead of exchange platforms, the stock is usually bought and sold over the counter. It has cheap share prices, typically under $1. Investors can buy multiple shares at once because to the affordable prices.

The investor gains a lot of money from selling the purchased shares as the stock price increases.

Speculative stock is typical in sectors including biotechnology, mining, and energy. Such industries have a high chance of success or failure since their price frequently undergoes significant, unanticipated changes.

Essentially, these are the main types of stocks that may be bought and sold on the stock market, however common and preferred stocks are the most well-liked. You may have observed that these stocks all center around similar issues. These factors include the company's size, sector, and trading strategy. Table 1 below summarizes how the two main categories differ from one another.

How Do Dividend Stocks Work?

We will provide you a comprehensive introduction to dividend stocks in this chapter. No prior understanding is required. We will briefly discuss dividend distributions and the operation of the stock market. We will also discuss the reasons why some stocks pay dividends while others do not, as well as how to identify the stocks that consistently pay high dividends. We'll also go over the fundamental principle of compound interest that underlies dividends. Compound interest is, however, much more effective for investors than savings accounts or other instruments because stocks themselves increase in value. It resembles compound interest on an energy kick.

Introduction to the Stock Market

Please bear with me as I provide a general overview of the stock market for those readers who are total newbies, to ensure that everyone is aware of the basics of stock investment.

During Europe's period of adventure in the 17th century, stock markets were created. Large sea vessels were being constructed at the time to "explore" distant regions in order to trade products. The little Netherlands, then a major world power, saw this industry really take off there. Ships from the Netherlands set out for Asia and Africa in search of expensive spices, silks, and other goods.

In those days, mounting abroad journeys like this was incredibly costly and quite perilous. A particular vessel's seaworthiness was quite likely to be compromised. While others would attempt to raise money by making appeals to the monarchs who at the time dominated the majority of European nations, Holland had a thriving and free economy. Some clever individuals came up with the concept of creating a corporation to organize international travel and offering parts, or shares, of the company to the general public. People could purchase shares to own a small fraction of the newly established Dutch East India Company after it started selling stock to the general public. They would be entitled to a proportionate share of the company's profits as part of their ownership.

Something generates a secondary market as soon as you sell it. The same applied to stocks. People started selling their shares to others instead of the company, frequently for a price higher than what they originally paid for them. The first stock markets were created during this time. Stock markets quickly developed into regulated locations where consumers could trade their shares. The current ideas of stock markets and trading emerged swiftly, with people making money not only from the company's revenues but also from increases in the share prices itself. The idea quickly expanded to other nations as other businesses began to issue stock shares.

Current Stock Market Structure and Dividends

Although the ideas that were formed at that time have not altered much, the idea of providing stock in a firm has grown, gotten regulated, and become more centralized over the ages. By the turn of the 20th century, there were established stock markets, such as the New York Stock Exchange, which was essential for stock sales. A publicly traded corporation as opposed to a privately held one became a concept. Anyone with the necessary funds can purchase shares of a publicly listed company's stock on one of the main stock exchanges. This is actually carried out through a brokerage, a business that offers the general public a way to open accounts used for trading stocks. You can put money into one of these accounts and use it to purchase or sell stock by placing orders. The brokerage actually executes the transactions on the stock exchanges on your behalf. Most businesses charge a small commission per transaction for this service.

Following the Great Depression, stock markets underwent extensive regulation. The newly established Securities and Exchange Commission in the United States carried out this function. Although it is difficult to assess whether the restrictions as a whole are protecting investors, they do offer some reassurance that publicly traded corporations are being truthful about their financial status. Companies are required by law to submit a number of audited reports that include information on their assets, liabilities, income, and earnings, among other things. These reports can be used to assess the company's financial standing and decide whether it is worthwhile to invest in. While this usually works, some businesses that were founded on deception, like WorldCom and Enron, manage to evade detection from time to time. However, those occurrences are extremely uncommon, and stock market openness has been preserved.

So let's discuss the dividends issue. What is a dividend, the most fundamental topic of all, should be addressed first? You may remember that during our consideration of the Dutch East India Company, it distributed proportionate percentages of its profits to those who held company stock. These distributions of profits are now referred to as dividends.

The basic answer to the question, "What is a dividend?" is that it is a payout of the firm's profits that you receive if you own stock in the company. Normally, dividends are given out every three months. You can research crucial details regarding a company's dividend payments to get a sense of how valuable it is to buy the shares. Things to think about are:

Dividend Payment: The dollar amount per share for the dividend payment. Therefore, you can check for a stock's yearly dividend payment to acquire a specific annual income from that investment. then calculate the required shareholding. If a firm pays a dividend of $4 per share, for instance, and you want to invest in the stock to earn $6,000 a year, you must own $6,000/$4 = 1,500 shares of the company's stock. Divide the given annual payment by four to get the amount you would earn with each quarterly dividend payment, keeping in mind that dividends are paid.

Yield is the same as "interest rate" for a savings account or certificate of deposit. However, yield is determined on a per-share basis. You may compute yield yourself by taking the dividend payment and dividing it by the stock price, which is how it is done on the majority of stock market websites. Take Abbvie (ABBV), for instance, which has a stock price of $65 and a dividend payment of $4.28 at the moment. The yield is 6.6% ($4.28) × ($65) x 100. However, take note that the majority of websites will quote the forward yield. The anticipated production for the following year is this. Changes in the anticipated dividend payout or variations in the stock price could have an impact on that. Those are estimates, of course, but you'll find that the present yield and the forward yield are quite similar.

Ex-Dividend Date: The corporation will announce a date for dividend payments each quarter. They will also announce a record date. On that day, dividend payments to shareholders are officially recorded. This takes into consideration share trading and establishes who is the rightful owner of the stock to receive payments. You must own the shares on the ex-Dividend date, which is normally two days prior to the date of record, in order for it to be recorded. There will be times when you need to sell shares of a dividend stock, but as a long-term investor you shouldn't be doing this frequently. Make sure that if you sell shares, you wait until the dividend payment has been made so that you receive that payment in order to avoid any unforeseen issues. If you plan to purchase shares, aim to do so before the ex-dividend date.

Dividends per share divided by earnings per share is known as the payout ratio. This offers you an idea of a company's capacity to maintain the existing level of dividend payments. Unless there are strong grounds to think that the situation may turn in your favor moving forward, you should avoid any company with a payout ratio that is close to, or worse, exceeds, a 100% payout ratio. The payout ratio for the pharmaceutical business Abbvie is 47%. This is a respectable number, indicating that the company can pay dividends and that there is plenty of space to raise dividend payments. When it comes to paying dividends, a company with a payout ratio of 90% or more is probably not going to be able to maintain the current dollar amount per share.

Dividend Growth: The number of years the dividend payment has climbed continuously. The better the investment, the more dividend growth years you see. For instance, Abbvie, a pharmaceutical business, has a 46-year dividend increase history. With such a strong track record, you should consider investing in the business to help protect your retirement income.

Finally, you must be aware of the share price. This will give you a rough sense of how much it will cost to receive the kind of income you're looking for for a specific dividend payment. Avoid searching for purported bargains because, in most situations, a low share price indicates that the stock is weak. However, when making your decisions, you must balance the share price with other considerations.

If you comprehend the topics covered in this section, you comprehend the fundamentals required to judge whether a certain dividend-paying company is a wise investment. Of course, there will be a lot more things to take into account; we'll talk about them in chapter 8 when we address fundamental analysis. In order to establish whether a firm is a good investment, this sort of research looks at the basics of the business, including profitability, inventories, assets, and liabilities.

Yield Matters, but Use Caution

Since the main goal of dividend stocks is interest rate income, you should look for a stock that has a high yield. But yield isn't the only thing to take into account. Average to slightly above average yields are what you want. This could be a warning sign if the yields are extremely high. Very high yields are frequently offered by stocks that are not suitable investments and are done so to lure investors to purchase shares of their underwhelming securities. Many equities, some as high as 15% or 18%, will have yields above 10%. These equities should be viewed in the same light as trash bonds. Although you can always sell your shares to exit a stock, you still need to find a buyer, thus it could be challenging to do so in the case of a stock you don't want. And if it hasn't already, the stock may drop at some point. Many stocks with extraordinarily high yields cost less than $10 per share; some are even penny stocks. A dividend investor ought to exercise caution, moderation, and procedure. This implies that you will likely refrain from investing in penny stocks, or at least you should. Focus on big, established, and mostly blue-chip enterprises. We will also discuss investing in exchange traded funds, which will increase your possibilities because the provider of the fund will reduce your risks by making simultaneous investments in dozens to hundreds of businesses.

Payments of Dividends in the Past

The history of a company's dividend payments is one item you'll want to look at. Are they increasing, decreasing, or steadfast? The preferred corporation pays increasing dividends. In a modern economy, we must continually fight against inflation, and if a dividend payout does not increase over time due to inflation, it is losing value. Therefore, unless there are some very good reasons from the fundamental research to anticipate that the situation is likely to change in the future, you definitely do not want a company with stagnant or declining dividend payments.

Another item to think about is how the business handled dividend payments during previous recessions. Investigate further if you discover that the business utilized a downturn as a pretext to reduce dividend payments. When the recession ended, did they immediately increase payments to the previous level? Or did they maintain dividend payments at a new, lower level while blaming the recession? During recessions, some businesses will maintain their dividend payments. These are unquestionably reliable businesses to invest in.

Stock Value

It is tempting to look for discounts. But since everything must be paid for somehow, if a stock has a cheap price per share, that suggests that it may not be the ideal investment. Consider investing in certain value stocks while looking for dividend stocks to consider. In chapter 4, we'll talk about what that actually implies. A low share price, however, does not signify "value" by itself. Avoid investing in stocks that are under $30 per share. There are some good stocks that might be less expensive, but they need to be carefully analyzed. Share prices of mature corporations that make solid investments often range from $50 to $100 or more per share.

Here's Why Not All Stocks Pay Dividends

Why certain stocks don't pay any dividends at all is one of the stock market's mysteries for novice dividend investors. These are frequently well-known and valuable stocks, such as Google, Netflix, or Amazon. What's happening here?

Do not forget what a dividend is. Investors receive a portion of the company's income, frequently the majority. The company must be mature, have significant worth, and have a firm hold on the market it operates in order to be in a position to do that. That in no way implies that it must be a monopoly, though. But it must have a strong, largely consistent market share. More importantly, it has to have a sizable enough market share to stop actively pursuing expansion. This might include market share both domestically and abroad, in other developed markets like Japan and Europe as well as mature markets.

Many older businesses are still expanding, but they do it slowly and steadily. They undoubtedly spend a lot of money on research and development, and they want to maintain their market share while expanding it sustainably. These firms are able to distribute dividends. This includes businesses like Microsoft, Apple, Apple, IBM, Amgen, Chevron, and Boeing.

Some businesses, however, are in a moment of rapid expansion. The likelihood that a corporation is pursuing very aggressive growth increases with age. These days, the majority (but not all) of high-tech businesses fall within this category. A few examples include Facebook, Google, Twitter, Tesla, and Amazon. These businesses invest each and every one of their revenues back into the business in order to expand quickly and capture new markets. They might even be losing money right now, just like Tesla and Amazon have for years. These businesses do not pay dividends because they spend every dollar that is received. Naturally, this does not imply that the stock is not worthwhile to own. The value of the stock in these companies has increased significantly, and is expected to do so for many more years, if not decades. They can therefore be a wise investment for various additional factors. And if you buy a lot of shares today, it might pay off later on when you sell them for a profit or perhaps when the firms get older and start paying dividends.

That kind of investment, however, is not the subject of this book. Finding firms that pay dividends and making investments in them are the main topics of this book. If increasing your dividend income is your primary objective, you should remain laser-focused and steer clear of stock investments based on assumptions. Even if there is a fair chance that many of the mentioned companies, like Netflix or Amazon, would likely increase in value over time and eventually pay dividends, these are both speculative and hence risky propositions. Contrarily, there is substantially less risk involved in investing in an established business that has a history of making good dividend payments and that is located in a promising evergreen industry.

How to Locate Stocks Paying Dividends

It is fairly simple to find stocks that pay dividends. You can check up stock tickers on any stock market website. The website will list specific share characteristics for each stock, such as the P/E ratio (price to earnings ratio). Other significant aspects of the stock, such as whether or not it pays dividends, will also be listed. When it comes to yield and payment, as well as ex-dividend date, if a corporation does not pay dividends, it will read N/A (not applicable). The stock pays dividends if the yield, payment, and ex-dividend date are listed.

You can also go to dividend.com, which is the top website in the world for locating stocks that pay dividends and analyzing important data about such firms, such as yield, share price, payout ratio, and yearly dividend payment. The majority of the key functions are provided without charge, but you must purchase a subscription to use all of the features. Additionally, you can access lists of dividend stocks, such as those offering the greatest yields or yearly dividends.

Building a sound portfolio made up of a diverse but constrained selection of investments is the way to go. We shall discuss investment methods in more detail later. In order to choose the companies you wish to invest in as part of your plan, you can use these websites along with fundamental analysis.

What Carry Out New Investors?

The number of advertisements for day traders, who purchase and sell shares in a matter of hours or even minutes, on the internet, social networks, and email inboxes is booming. They are the same folks who treat you like a loser if you don't buy into whatever get-rich-quick program they are pitching to you. But they are only salespeople; they are nothing more. All they are doing is whacking at your brain's primitive regions that want you to feel dread all the time with a metaphorical bat.

It is now referred to as FOMO (Fear of Missing Out). The same cognitive process makes you constantly check your phone to see who has done what on the newest video platform or who has liked or disliked your dating profile. But keep in mind that this isn't how the slothful investor invests. We employ reason and data. perseverance and patience. When it comes to investing in the markets, "indifference" is actually our most crucial emotion.

There is no reason to ever change what you do as a new or seasoned investor once you realize why passive investing, the strategy of long-term perseverance and indifference to short-term market fluctuations, can be more profitable than anything those slick-haired day traders are trying to get you to buy for just four easy monthly payments.

Don't rely just on my word, though. Let's instead look at why this is the case. Numerous studies have demonstrated that psychological tendencies control humans in every aspect of life. Many of these characteristics can increase the risk of making mistakes, and trust me when I say investing mistakes are painful mistakes. For example, if you have a chocolate ice cream addiction or spend money on lottery tickets and nightly blackjack games, you may be more likely to make blunders. These flaws cause problems that prevent potential good investors from participating in the market and earning the profits they deserve.

Yes, making investments in the stock market can be risky. At times, you succeed. Occasionally, you don't. However, if you approach it properly, based on facts, and with patience, it will appear less like a gamble and more like an informed investment decision.

Reality or Emotions?

What distinguishes fact from emotion in the realm of investing? It's fairly easy.

Facts are founded in history. Future-related feelings are present.

Financial media articles are frequently filled by the investment world's gamblers, who mistakenly combine facts and emotions. "Pfizer is your best investment because viruses are here to stay," or "I bought Apple stock because it's the future!""

With the iPhone and other goods, Apple (Ticker: AAPL) has undoubtedly had a huge impact on our daily lives. However, who is to say that another tech company won't innovate more quickly and eventually overtake Apple in terms of consumer base?

And yeah, it's true that viruses won't actually go away any time soon, but can you say for sure that a young genius won't come up with a treatment for every disease?

It's wonderful to be optimistic about the possibility of these events occurring, but it's quite another to view the situation objectively, as a lazy investor.

The sole reliable investor is...

Let me demonstrate how bad humans are at investing, but I should warn you that it will be extremely embarrassing.

I discussed why the owner of the investment portfolio is the portfolio's biggest opponent in the previous few pages.

The missing punchline for the header of this section is "...a dead investor," therefore being a passive investor, which is defined as one who doesn't excessively monitor their portfolio, is a decent investment strategy.

This embarrassing one-liner was said with just a hint of humor because it turned out to be sort of true later on.

Fidelity, a global investment manager, conducted a study to determine which accounts performed the best overall. The findings revealed two investor categories that outperformed every other account holder:

Investors who failed to remember they had Fidelity accounts.

the deceased investors.

It's precisely why you should embrace sloth and turn into a passive (lazy!) investor since lazy investors, by their very nature, do not interfere with their investments, whether it's a cheesy one-liner or the findings of an actual commissioned study.

You can't find a more passive income source than an index-based ETF investment portfolio; it requires very little work on your part. This is the real marvel of the markets, and the most efficient way to enjoy the fruits of accrued interest without any special knowledge or effort. Unlike your paycheck, for which you work very hard, your investment portfolio is passive income.

Buy and Hold.

John C. Bogle, founder of the Vanguard Group, is one of my financial heroes because he developed one of the first exchange-traded funds (ETFs). In fact, I thought about hanging a picture of him in our bedroom, but my wife had other ideas (namely, anything but hanging a picture of my financial hero in our bedroom), but that's a story for another book.

Back to my point: Mr. Bogle was a big proponent of common-sense investing, and one of his eight basic rules for investors was to "Buy & Hold" an investment strategy. However, despite how sensible it may seem, investors who choose Bogle's "Buy & Hold" investment strategy should be aware that it does come with some market volatility over time. Let me explain.

Be Ready for Slight Turns!

Crises will occasionally affect the markets, resulting in graphs that show the rising and falling prices of indices, as well as the ebb and flow of the national mood. While sharp market declines are common talk among the active (cowboy) investors, lazy investors like us - who have our money in a diverse basket of securities - don't care about these sharp turns. They will...all the time. But we can ride i.

The ability of humanity to overcome hardship has been demonstrated repeatedly throughout history. For instance, in 1815, when the Indonesian volcano Mount Tambora erupted and plunged the entire planet into a year-long winter, trade relations were maintained and today, no one even remembers that year when summer didn't happen.

I put my faith in the markets' capacity to develop and expand since, on a similar scale, people and societies have always discovered innovative methods to make money, regardless of war, natural disasters, or worldwide pandemics.

It's true that some years will produce investment managers who confidently announce they "beat the market" but as long as they haven't provided proof of their ability to predict the future, it's probably just plain luck. When you, as an investor, purchase ETFs that track leading indices, you are actually expressing your confidence in the market as a whole.

Statistically, if there are many investors in the market, inevitably, about half of all invested capital will see an above-average performance, and the other half will show below-average performance. If all investments around the world have certain average growth rates, then in a particular year, some investments will yield above-average profits. It may even happen over two, three, or even five years — this is just called statistics.

The process of taking a result and, in reverse, examining each of the steps leading to the successful final result is commonly referred to as "Reverse Engineering".

The facts—not the feelings—are that very few investors—2%, to be exact—have historically produced returns that have exceeded the average return of the market during periods of fifteen years or longer.

There are winners and losers in every statistical analyses.

You don't need to be a genius to take the elevator to the top floor, but anyone who invested in the entire market that year actually admitted to never anticipating these unusual developments. Throughout the COVID-19 pandemic in 2020, not only were technology company profits unaffected by globally imposed social distancing measures, they actually went up — a lot.

Since you are probably not a skilled investor, investing in stocks will benefit you in the long run, but only if two requirements are satisfied:

No, five years is not enough time for your investment timetable.

Your assets are quite diverse, ideally in a diversified stock index that includes numerous businesses that operate in a variety of industry areas.

While it can be challenging to stay indifferent in times of crisis if the value of equities is plunging, indifference is like a muscle – you must train it to make it stronger.

Losing $3,000 in a week of trading was very difficult to hear back then, but at the same time, in hindsight, this event was an excellent lesson that taught me to take my finger off the investment trigger before making a fatal mistake - a fear-based sale at a loss. I still remember the feeling of horror and grief when I saw my portfolio cut to half its size back in 2008, when I was nineteen.

Benny, Kenny, and Jenny's Story of Investing with Indifference

I'd like to introduce you to Benny, Kenny, and Jenny, all long-term investors in the security markets, but each has a distinct investing "personality" (they may or may not be real persons, but that doesn't matter).

Their financial tales span a 40-year time span, from roughly 1980 (I can have Gen X buddies!) through just before the COVID-19 global pandemic in early 2020, when market changes were known to be impacted by:

Black Monday (1987): 20% decline in the stock market

Kuwait War (1991): investors lost 20% of their money.

Leading indices lost 50% of their value during the Dot-com crisis of 2000, and it took years for them to recover.

The US subprime real estate crisis of 2008 saw a 50% decline in market prices on a global scale.

Let's now examine how each of Benny, Kenny, and Jenny managed their investments over the course of those 40 years.

Kenny

Kenny, the most anxious of the three friends, put $2,500 of his pay into his bank account each month, but every time he plucked up the courage to invest it, KABOOM, a globally catastrophic event exploded off the front pages of newspapers all over the world — raging wars, real estate dives, bursting industry bubbles. Inevitably, the stock market took the same catastrophic tumble.

Benny

Having just graduated from the College of Fast-Easy-Money in 1980, Benny immediately developed an addiction to newspaper financial headline analysis — if only to satisfy his insatiable thirst for beating the market at its own game. He saved $2,500 every month, but waited until the exact moment when he felt the market was in a dip, and close to trending back up. Guess what — he succeeded! Unbelievably, Benny was able to sense when the markets were about to take off again.

Benny, like Kenny, over the years invested roughly $1.2 million. How did Benny make out after four amazing decades? Patience...we're getting there. After 40 years, Benny was exhausted and decided to take early retirement.

Jenny

Jenny was told the S&P 500 was her best bet when she first started investing with little to no knowledge of the markets, and that she should just set it up to automatically invest every month with the exact same amount — $2,500 — of her monthly salary. Jenny is a very busy woman, the marketing director at a well-known global guitar manufacturer, and she volunteers twice a month at the local seniors residence.

For the next forty years, as soon as her paycheck came in or was deposited, the pre-arranged amount would immediately be transferred to her investment portfolio and then used to purchase more units from the index-tracing ETFs. Jenny had no interest in the financial news or the short-term ups and downs of the market. She set that up to happen with her bank "automagically", and from that day on, it was like that $2,500 a month never even existed.

To the present day

Yes, even Kenny managed to part with some of his money and put it into an ETF. Over the four decades, Benny, Kenny, and Jenny invested their money in the stock market through various methodologies that all tracked the S&P 500 index. During this forty-year period, all three friends only bought stocks. None of them sold — not even nervous Kenny.

The outcomes!

Benny

Despite his seemingly reckless investing strategy, Benny still managed to reap the rewards and profits of some very successful companies, all of which were listed on the S&P 500. He never sold a single investment, but instead always invested his money just before any significant market collapse. In his old age, Benny decided to sell his investment portfolio for just over $1 million.

Kenny

Kenny had an investment portfolio at the time of its sale valued at $1,922,480 — a far larger return than Benny's! It turns out that flawless timing like Kenny's is a very successful asset when it comes to investing!

Jenny

When the year 2020 finally came, Jenny discovered how to use her phone to create an alert to notify her when it was time to "sell investment portfolio...time to reap the gains!She was shocked to discover when she first started her investment portfolio that the value of her holdings had grown to $2,030,610, surpassing Kenny's!

2020 investment portfolios for the three investors

Lessons Discovered

Even in the worst case scenario, if you invest your money effectively and let it work for itself, you could still be able to turn a profit.

Investors who are steady and unflappable are more likely to achieve larger returns than the majority of active and experienced investors.

No matter how large short-term market changes may appear to be at the time, buy ETFs that track stock indices frequently and hold onto them for decades!

Underlying Life Principles According To Warren Buffett

All throughout the world, ears perk up when Warren Buffet speaks on stock markets, business ethics, or the cost of corn in Nebraska. He frequently speaks about things that are not immediately pressing. Buffett's remarks appear to have an impact on many areas of our lives. Buffett is among the world's wealthiest individuals, but according to his buddy Charlie Munger, he is also one of the happiest people he knows. Consequently, I have chosen to include this chapter so that, before reading what Buffett has to say about successful investing, you might learn his ideas into living purposefully and contently.

Live your life as you see fit, including engaging in hobbies.

"Working with securities appealed to me in part because you could go about your daily life." It's not necessary to dress professionally.

We are what we eat, hence Buffett has always eaten only American food.

The result of a hugely successful party held to commemorate my fifth birthday, where we had hot dogs, hamburgers, soft drinks, popcorn, and ice cream, my attitudes about food and diet were indelibly set quite young.

Buffett's specialty dish is a dusty sundae, which he makes by drizzling a ton of malted milk powder and Hershey's chocolate syrup over vanilla ice cream. He provides a mathematical defense of the calories:

The amount of calories this mixture consumes is negligible. If your basal metabolic rate is 2,800 calories per day, then you can (and must) consume somewhat more than 1 million calories annually, according to simple math. For me, this means that I must consume about 25 million calories daily to prevent starvation-related mortality. Why not just do it?"

But sometimes the cost of calories isn't worth it. At a dinner party, Buffett was once presented with a glass of expensive wine. He responded, "No, thanks," while placing his palm over his glass. I'll accept cash.

In contrast, he spends his free time playing the card game of Bridge with friends and family, likening locating a suitable acquisition to a "bagging area and fast-moving elephants." Additionally, he joins family and friends for exceptional events like Bill Gates' wedding on the Hawaiian island of Lanai and an award awarded to his daughter by the Omaha YWCA for her work on the Rose Theater. He plans a gathering of his closest and oldest friends, the Buffett group, every other year. He stopped playing racquetball due to a back injury, although he still occasionally lays gold. He added that he started using a treadmill to exercise after seeing he had lost weight during an event.

Focus on your objectives and set high standards for them.

A shareholder questioned him during a Berkshire Hathaway annual meeting: "Now that you are the richest man in America, what's your next goal?"That's simple," Buffett said. becoming the senior citizen of America.

I look about for one-foot bars that I can step over rather than attempting to jump over seven-foot bars.

Buffett advises investors to approach investing like a hockey pro. If you want to swim 100 meters quickly, it is better to swim with the tide than to work on your stroke, as Wayne Gretzky famously advised.

"If we take the mainline from New York to Chicago, we don't get off at Altoona and go on side trips."

"I've frequently thought that studying company failures rather than business successes could be more beneficial. Business success cases are frequently studied in business schools. But my partner, Charlie Munger, claims that the only thing he is interested in is his own death, so he will never go there.

Putting off gratification

"Just putting one foot in front of the other every day has a lot to recommend it,"

The Three Little Pigs tale is one that we are all familiar with. The first and second young pigs in this story about maturity and impulse control spend the majority of their time playing, which is what kids do best. They take their adult obligations seriously, which would make them put off the enjoyment that comes from playing. They quickly and halfheartedly put together straw- and stick-based homes for one and the other. The third little pig, who appears less amusing but is portrayed as having maturity in the story, spends his time creating a safe haven for them all (the house of bricks). He enjoys having fun just as much as his brothers, without a doubt. But what makes him unique in maturity and ability to handle the hardships of the world (or the wolf) is his ability to put off having fun. The term "investing" indicates that what you do now is closely related to what you will do tomorrow and that the results of your labor today may not be immediately apparent.

Having the ability to postpone gratification is necessary for choosing investing as a means of support. Like the third small pig, investors must put in significant current effort in order to reap rewards in the future, even at the expense of pleasure today. There is no doubt that you must possess the characteristics of the third little pig if you want to be a great investor. In Warren Buffett's words, investing means "Forgoing consumption now to have the ability to consume more at a later date." For Buffett, it's not just a simple matter of postponing pleasure. He appears to have a sizable capacity to postpone it for extended periods of time. Prices can change dramatically over short time periods, and people may buy and sell different enterprises as a result of a wide range of emotions. Beyond his ability to make wise valuation decisions, his capacity to hold equities for extended periods of time enables him to wait for the more correct values of these companies to emerge.

We are born with a flurry of desires and urgent wants that at first seem impossible to suppress. If we're lucky, we grow up and reach a point where we can put off short-term gratification in favor of long-term objectives, such as giving up some pleasures that harm the environment in order to preserve it for future generations or reducing spending now in order to provide for their financial security. The concepts of the "Id," "ego," and "super ego" developed by Freud are helpful analogies for comprehending the motivation behind the want for fulfillment. The 'Id' is an irrational, impulsive, and untamed need to have one's demands met right away. It has no self-control and only cares about getting what it wants now. It resembles an uncontrollably greedy animal that ignores everyone and everything in order to satisfy its own demands. It is irrational desire. The superego is at the other extreme.

The perfectionistic, moralistic superego represents the highest social values and demands a flawless, pure life. To the demon of the Id, it is god. The processes that take place and the maturity needed to have any ability to postpone gratification are well-illustrated by Freud's model. As a result, it is clear that Buffett has a big ego and can handle disagreement in a cool-headed manner. He isn't under the control of a vindictive superego that snaps at him when he doesn't succeed right away. Equally, he is not propelled in either direction by an impulsive Id that demands that all of its requirements be met right away. Being Buffett requires an especially robust ego to control the appearance of desperation. A quality that appears to escape time and space is desperation. It distorts and obliterates the more mature and softer aspects of the personality; it seems to thrive on haste, impairs judgment, and feeds off of urgency.

It reduces things to their bare necessities in order to calm whatever one is desperate for. There isn't enough space or time to think clearly or to consider the effects of the action at hand. When something is desperate, there is a fear of missing out or losing. Extreme internal pressures that are perceived as inevitable seem to give rise to desperation. These needs turn to and center on a hyper-valued object, whose worth may be displaced (as with a specific type of affluent man who is still desperately seeking to increase his fortune) or genuine (as with a starving person desiring a cup of rice). Once sparked, this elusive desire can provide great excitement due to the possibility of fulfillment. An almost-emergency-like sense of excitement and urgency is produced by the scent of fulfillment, and the target of the desperation is chased with unwavering single-mindedness.

This makes it difficult to see the need for control and the danger to oneself or others. Buffett's ego strength enables him to control the intensity of his vital participation and excitement in the demanding world of investment without ever succumbing to desperation. Few people possess this ability. You must develop the ability to control your anxiety if you want to avoid feeling desperate but postpone gratification. Being able to hold worries and anxieties without trying to eliminate, replace, or reject them through action is what it means to contain anxiety. It is the ability to withstand unpredictability without losing control or becoming bankrupt too soon. It's a place where you can live without knowing the solution and where you can put up with tension while waiting for the solution to appear. When anxiety is effectively managed, one has the capacity to avoid disintegrating, panicking, or becoming frantic, and, perhaps most importantly, one does not resort to a variety of anxiety-related defense mechanisms.

This gives you the opportunity to consider your worries and reach a more sensible and well-informed decision. This is Buffett's strategy. One of the key elements of the capacity to postpone satisfaction is the ability to control anxiety. A lack of desperation and a robust ego are the two aspects of emotional maturity that are extremely supportive of the ability to postpone gratification. These factors all work together to affect Buffett's investment approach. The emotional strain his investment technique placed on him would be impossible without them. His phrase, "Intelligent expansion or acquisition opportunities...," captures this dynamic. When the debt market is oppressive, are most likely to appear. This displays his readiness to thwart the desire to earn the maximum returns on his money at all times, but wait till the elephant walks through. Our main premise is that, if you want to shoot, rare, fast-moving elephants, you need always carry a loaded rifle.

It is extremely challenging to get loans in order to undertake acquisitions when the financial market is oppressive. When he says, "There's much to be said for just putting one foot ahead of the other every day [in a steady unrushed way]," Buffett's mature down-to-earth way of being, especially when compared with others who invest large sums of money, is well-captured. This action can lead to significant financial advantages and happens to have an important mathematical edge over a more frenzied approach. "Imagine that Berkshire had only $1, which we put in a security that doubled by year's end and was then sold," Buffett uses an exaggerated hypothetical. Imagine further that we repeated this procedure with after-tax earnings every year for the ensuing 19 years, scoring a doubling each time. At the conclusion of the twenty-year period, the 34% capital gains tax we would have paid on the sales proceeds would have given the government around $13,000, leaving us with about $25,250. Very good.

However, our dollar would increase to $1,048,576 if we made a single excellent investment that, in turn, doubled twenty times over the course of twenty years. It is evident that significant obstacles must be overcome and significant personal traits must be in place in order to overcome impulsiveness. If we were to cash out, we would pay a 34% tax of around $356,500 and would then have approximately $692,000. If these attributes are lacking, they will undoubtedly become painfully apparent in a scenario where there is a sharp rise or fall in pricing. When there is a lot of money at stake, situations like this frequently lead to desperation, uncontrollable anxiety, and rash decisions. Buffett's ability to suppress worry and postpone gratification, however, really shines in his counterintuitive response to the scenario of declining stock values. "If the business continues to satisfy us, we welcome lower market prices of the stocks we own as an opportunity to acquire even more of a good thing at a better price."

Buffett remains calm.

Frugality

"Jack arrived after the scheduled time to close the sale at Charlie's office. He explained that he had been searching for a parking meter with some remaining time before finally arriving. For me, that was a truly amazing time. At that point, I realized Jack was going to be the manager I liked.

Does excessive riches require you to live frugally? Is it true that by keeping track of your pennies, your pounds will take care of themselves? Buffett is among the best of the penny pinchers, that much is certain. The complete opposite of giving in to our desires is being frugal. This contrasts with temperance, which calls for striking a balance between satisfying your wants and forgoing others. Extreme frugalness forbids impulsive behavior and the pursuit of happiness. It is more about suppressing impulses than it is about controlling them. Buffett is not looking at a man who is depriving himself when he is thrilled to encounter a man he feels is his sort of man—a man who is late for a meeting because he is driving around hunting for an unattended parking meter. He is observing a man who is fully immersed in what is important to him—saving money.

Buffett views the perceived frugalness of the parking meter man as a virtue primarily in symbolic terms because it has nothing to do with really saving money. A businessman of that caliber can generate significantly more income in the next fifteen minutes than he can by avoiding paying the parking meter. Therefore, it is about a whole way of being—the value of money is ingrained in his personality and his perception of what is important in life. Buffett and many others advocate against making purchases purely for the purpose of making them. His appeal to these thrifty folks, in particular their aversion to spending money, is successful. They are the kind of people who, while employed by his firms, would refrain from making superfluous purchases, assisting him in realizing his ultimate objective of amassing as much capital as he could.

So instead of being primarily about self-denial, the type of so-called frugality we are looking at in Buffett is more about a commitment to refrain from spending money pointlessly so that it might be accumulated. Some people may become so emotionally invested in not spending that it severely limits their ability to use their money in innovative ways to generate additional income. With Buffett, this is clearly not the case. Buffett's primary driving force in life is to acquire and amass wealth, which keeps him from paying an unaffordable price for his extreme financial austerity.

In reality, there is absolutely no cost to be paid because, by depriving himself of the pleasures that money might provide, he is actually enhancing the ultimate pleasure by compounding the growth of the money that would have otherwise been spent in search of momentary gratification.

Buffett views being thrifty as an extravagant, incredibly reassuring, and symbolic gesture. Knowing that others aren't overindulging makes him feel good. Buffett is a collector unlike any other because, above all, he wants to amass as much cash as he can. It's interesting that Buffett has access to the constraint that comes with being thrifty on many different levels. It encourages a responsible, methodical approach to investment, which has greatly aided in his success. Buffett's single-minded emphasis on amassing wealth probably has a relationship to such strong emotional aspects of his life that being thrifty to do so is satisfying important and deeply-felt desires.

Why run the risk?

"In my opinion, Ronald Reagan was correct when he said, "Hard work never killed anyone, but why take the chance?"

Humans have a propensity for being picky and an inclination toward making decisions. We don't take use of all the opportunities or resources that are presented to us. From the options offered, we pick what is most desirable. Even if this is a normal aspect of being human, it is also this that plants the initial seeds for the emergence of jealousy. Buffett does not suffer from the same sensation of lack or self-deficiency as those who are envious of others do. He does not have an idealized self that is out of reach. He has no desire to pretend to be someone imposing that he is not, nor does he want for others' outstanding traits that he lacks. Instead of idealizing the traits he admires in people like Benjamin Graham, he absorbs, digests, and integrates them in a more realistic manner. He can let them be their authentic selves while still getting strength from their presence without taking them into himself. Buffett pursues his goals because he believes he can achieve them and does so.

He doesn't long for something he can't have though because he is aware of this. For instance, we are aware of his love for making money, preferably a lot of it. The fact that he understood that wasn't his area of expertise prevented him from being tempted to join the "gold rush" during the entire dot-com boom as he watched others make outrageous sums of money. Buffett doesn't experience the kind of lack that many of us are prone to; he accepts himself and his limitations realistically and is aware that he is just Warren Buffett and not George Soros, Julian Robertson, or Donald Trump. The freedom he now has to exist in his own universe and pay attention to the tasks at hand is tremendous. It distinguishes him from the rest of us who devote a great deal of mental energy to our obsession with rivals and those we think are superior to us. In a world full with distractions, it allows him to maintain outstanding attention.

He beautifully expressed his honest admiration for others when he added, "In fairness, we've seen plenty of achievements as well, some very exceptional. I have a lot of respect for numerous executives at large corporations, including Ken Chenault of American Express, Jeff Immelt of General Electric, and Dick Kovacevich of Wells Fargo. However, I don't believe I could handle their level of management. And I'm aware that I wouldn't enjoy a lot of the responsibilities that go along with their jobs, including meetings, speeches, international travel, the charity circuit, and working with governments. I believe Ronald Reagan was correct when he said, "Hard work probably doesn't kill anyone, but why take the chance?As a result, I've chosen the simple path of doing nothing but watching excellent managers run their shows. My only responsibilities are to support them, develop and strengthen our corporate culture, and make important capital allocation choices. Our managers have honored this trust by exerting themselves and performing well.

The capacity to recognize others' accomplishments might be viewed as the antidote to envy. Buffett, though, excels at this and goes beyond merely praising them. He doesn't have to reduce them in size in order to use them for his own gain. Then, he goes above and beyond simply leaving them undamaged; he shields, inspires, and liberates them so that they can be superior to himself. He is free from the constant internal pain of merely being good and not better since he is not enviously connected with them. Buffett is happy to have them around because he is aware that he is not they and doesn't want to be them. He remains in his skin, with all its advantages and disadvantages, with his sense of self covered by a thick membrane. Buffett is fully aware of this and is also aware that much of his success stems from his ability to recognize and take advantage of the significant benefits of others.

When Warren Buffet discusses the stock market, corporate ethics, or the price of maize in Nebraska, ears perk up all over the world. He usually discusses topics that are not urgent right away. The comments Buffett made seem to have an effect on many aspects of our existence. Buffett is one of the wealthiest persons in the world, but his friend Charlie Munger claims that he is also one of the happiest people he knows. As a result, I decided to include this chapter so that you might discover Buffett's perspectives on living a purposeful and happy life before reading what he has to say about successful investing.

Enjoy your life the way you see fit, including your interests.

It's not required to dress professionally. "Working with securities appealed to me in part because you could go about your daily life."

Buffett has always eaten exclusively American food because we are what we eat.

My opinions regarding food and diet were indeliably formed pretty young as a result of a hugely successful party arranged to celebrate my fifth birthday, when we had hot dogs, hamburgers, soft drinks, popcorn, and ice cream.

Buffett's signature dish is a dusty sundae, which he prepares by spreading a ton of Hershey's chocolate syrup and malted milk powder over vanilla ice cream. He offers the following mathematical support for the calories:

This combo contains hardly any calories at all. You can (and must) consume somewhat more than 1 million calories annually if your basal metabolic rate is 2,800 calories per day. For me, this means that I need to eat around 25 million calories every day to avoid dying from famine. Just do it, why wait?"

However, occasionally the expense of calories is not justified. Buffett once received a glass of pricey wine at a dinner gathering. "No, thanks," he said, laying his hand over his glass in reply. Cash is acceptable.

He joins family and friends for exceptional events like Bill Gates' wedding on the Hawaiian island of Lanai and a prize given to his daughter by the Omaha YWCA for her work on the Rose Theater, but spends his free time playing the card game of Bridge with friends and family, comparing the search for a suitable acquisition to a "bagging area and fast-moving elephants." Every other year, Jimmy organizes a get-together for his closest and oldest pals, the Buffett group. Due to a back problem, he was forced to stop playing racquetball, however he still occasionally lays gold. He continued by saying that he began using a treadmill to workout after seeing he had lost weight while participating in an event.

Concentrate on your goals and hold them to a high standard.

During a Berkshire Hathaway annual meeting, a shareholder asked Buffett, "Now that you are the richest man in America, what's your next goal? "Buffett said, "That's simple. becoming the senior citizen of America.

Instead of attempting to jump over seven-foot bars, I seek around for 1-foot bars that I can step over.

If you want to swim 100 meters swiftly, it is better to swim with the tide than to focus on your stroke, as Wayne Gretzky famously suggested. Buffett recommends investors to approach investing like a hockey great.

"If we take the mainline from New York to Chicago, we don't get off at Altoona and take side trips."

"I've often considered that studying business failures rather than business successes could be more advantageous. Business schools typically study examples of successful businesses. However, my companion Charlie Munger insists that his primary interest is in dying, therefore he won't go there.

delaying gratification

There is much to be said for just placing one foot in front of the other each day.

We are all familiar with the story of the Three Little Pigs. In this tale of maturity and impulse control, the first and second young pigs spend the majority of their time playing, which is what children do best. They put off the delight of playing because they take their responsibilities as adults seriously. For one another, they hurriedly and clumsily constructed dwellings out of sticks and straw. The third little pig, who in the story is depicted as being more mature but who is less entertaining, spends his time building a safe haven for them all (the house of bricks). He certainly enjoys having fun just as much as his brothers do. But his capacity to put off having fun sets him apart from other people in terms of maturity and his capacity to deal with challenges in life (or the wolf).

The word "investing" implies that what you do now will have a significant impact on what you will do tomorrow and that your efforts today might not yield instant rewards.

To choose investing as a source of support, one must be able to put off getting what one wants. Investors must put in significant current effort, even at the price of enjoyment today, to receive dividends in the future, just like the third small pig. It goes without saying that if you want to be a successful investor, you must have the traits of the third tiny pig. For Warren Buffett, it's not just a matter of delaying pleasure; he defines investing as "Forgoing consumption now to have the ability to consume more at a later date." He seems to be able to delay it for long periods of time in a significant way. Prices can fluctuate sharply in brief periods of time, and people may buy and sell various businesses as a response of a wide range of emotions. In addition to his aptitude for making prudent valuation choices, his capacity for holding stocks for protracted periods of time helps him to wait for the more accurate values of these companies to emerge.

We are born with a whirlwind of needs and desires that at first seem difficult to smother. If we're lucky, as we get older, we can learn to put off our immediate desires in favor of long-term goals, such as avoiding certain pleasures that harm the environment in order to protect it for future generations or cutting back on spending now in order to ensure their financial security. To understand the motive underlying the need for fulfillment, Freud's ideas of the "Id," "ego," and "super ego" are useful analogies. The 'Id' is an unbridled, unreasonable desire to have one's wants met immediately. It lacks restraint and is just concerned with receiving what it wants right away. It resembles a beast with uncontrollable greed that disregards everyone and everything to fulfill its own needs. This desire is irrational. At the other extreme is the superego.

The moralistic, perfectionistic superego, which seeks a perfect, pure life, stands for the highest social values. It is god to the devil of the Id. Freud's model does a good job of illuminating the steps that must be taken as well as the level of maturity required to be able to delay gratification. As a result, it is evident that Buffett has a large ego and is capable of handling conflict rationally. He doesn't have a vengeful superego that snaps at him when he doesn't achieve his goals straight away. He is also not driven by an impetuous Id that requires that all of its demands be fulfilled immediately in either direction. To avoid coming across as desperate, Buffett needs to have a very strong ego. Desperation is a quality that seems to transcend place and time. The more refined and gentler components of the personality are distorted and destroyed; it seems to thrive on speed, impede judgment, and be fueled by urgency.

In order to calm whatever one is in desperate need of, it strips things down to their essential needs. There isn't enough time or room to think rationally or to weigh the pros and disadvantages of the current course of action. A fear of losing or missing out arises when something is desperate. Desperation appears to be caused by extremely high internal pressures that are thought to be inevitable. These demands focus on and revolve around a hyper-valued object, whose value may be shifted (as in the case of a particular sort of wealthy guy who is still desperately trying to grow his wealth) or genuine (as in the case of someone who is starving and wants a cup of rice). The potential of realizing this elusive ambition can be very exciting once it's ignited. The scent of fulfillment creates an almost emergency-like sense of exhilaration and urgency, and the object of the desperation is pursued with unyielding single-mindedness.

It becomes challenging to recognize the need for control and the risk to oneself or others as a result. Buffett's ego power allows him to maintain self-control over the depth of his essential involvement and joy in the tough world of investing without ever giving in to desperation. Few people have this talent. If you want to stop feeling hopeless but postpone gratification, you must learn how to control your worry. To contain anxiety is to be able to hold fears and anxieties without attempting to replace, reject, or erase them through action. It is the capacity for enduring uncertainty without slipping out of control or becoming bankrupt too quickly. It's a location where you can exist without knowing the answer and where you can tolerate stress as you wait for the answer to materialize. Effective anxiety management gives one the ability to prevent collapsing, panicking, or getting hysterical, and, perhaps most critically, it prevents one from using a number of anxiety-related defense mechanisms.

This provides you the chance to think about your concerns and make a more sane and informed decision. This is Buffett's plan of action. The ability to manage worry is one of the essential components of the capability to postpone satisfaction. The two characteristics of emotional maturity that are most supportive of the capacity to postpone fulfillment are a lack of desperation and a strong ego. All of these elements interact to influence Buffett's investment strategy. Without them, he couldn't have endured the emotional toll his investment method took. The way he puts it, "Intelligent expansion or acquisition opportunities...," perfectly expresses this dynamic. are most likely to manifest themselves when the loan market is onerous. This demonstrates his willingness to thwart the impulse to always obtain the most profits on his investment, but hold off until the elephant enters the room. Our major argument is that you must constantly carry a loaded gun if you want to shoot rare, moving elephants.

In an oppressive financial market, it is very difficult to obtain loans in order to make acquisitions. Buffett's mature down-to-earth attitude is well-captured when he says, "There's much to be said for just putting one foot ahead of the other every day [in a steady unrushed way]," especially when compared to other investors who make tremendous sums of money. This move has a considerable mathematical advantage over a more frantic approach and can result in substantial financial benefits. Buffett proposes an overblown hypothetical: "Imagine that Berkshire had only $1, which we invested in a security that doubled by year's end and was then sold." Suppose moreover that we carried on this technique with after-tax earnings each year for the subsequent 19 years, doubling our money each time. The 34% capital gains tax we would have paid on the sales profits at the end of the twenty-year period would have given the government around $13,000, leaving us with about $25,250. Very impressive.

However, if we made a single, exceptional investment that, in turn, increased twenty times over the period of twenty years, our dollar would increase to $1,048,576. Evidently, overcoming impulsiveness requires major character traits to be in place as well as big hurdles to be overcome. If we cashed out, we would have about $690,000 after paying a 34% tax on about $356,500. If any of these qualities are lacking, it is certain that a scenario in which there is a rapid spike or fall in pricing will make them painfully evident. Situations like this typically result in desperation, overwhelming anxiety, and hasty decisions when there is a lot of money at stake. Buffett, however, really demonstrates his capacity for restraint and deferral in his unexpected response to the scenario of falling stock prices. We embrace reduced market prices of the stocks we own as a chance to buy even more of a good thing at a better price if the business continues to satisfy us.

Buffett doesn't flinch.

Frugality

For me, that was a very great moment when I recognized Jack was going to be the manager I liked. He stated that he had been looking for a parking meter with some remaining time before eventually arriving that he had come after the allocated time to close the sale at Charlie's office.

The complete opposite of giving in to our desires is being frugal, which contrasts with temperance, which calls for striking a balance between satisfying your wants and foregoing others. Extreme frugalness forbids impulsive behavior and the pursuit of happiness. Buffett is among the best of the penny pinchers, that much is certain.

A businessman of that caliber can generate significantly more income in the next fifteen minutes than he can by not paying the parking meter, so it is about a whole way of being—the value of money is ingrained in his personality and his perception of what is important in life. Buffett and many others see the perceived thriftiness of the parking meter man as a virtue primarily in symbolic terms.

The type of so-called frugality we are looking at in Buffett is more about a commitment to refrain from spending money mindlessly so that it might be accumulated, rather than being primarily about self-denial as some people may become emotionally invested in not spending that it severely limits their ability to use their money in creative ways to generate additional income.

Buffett is a collector unlike any other because, above all, he wants to accumulate as much money as he can. It's interesting that Buffett has access to the constraint that comes with being thrifty on many different levels. It encourages a responsible, methodical approach to investment, which has greatly aided in his success. Buffett sees being thrifty as an extravagant, incredibly reassuring, and symbolic gesture. Knowing that others aren't overindulging makes him feel good.

Why take the chance?

Ronald Reagan was right, in my opinion, when he remarked, "Hard work never killed anyone, but why take the chance?"

Buffett does not experience the same sense of lack or self-deficiency as those who are envious of others do.

Buffett doesn't experience the kind of lack that many of us are prone to; he accepts himself and his limitations. For example, we are aware of his love for making money, preferably a lot of it. The fact that he understood that wasn't his area of expertise prevented him from being tempted to join the "gold rush" during the entire dot-com boom as he watched others make outrageous sums of money.

He continued, "In fairness, we've seen lots of successes as well, some really extraordinary, and that eloquently reflected his sincere love for others. Many leaders at big companies, like Ken Chenault of American Express, Jeff Immelt of General Electric, and Dick Kovacevich of Wells Fargo, I have a lot of respect for. I don't think I could manage their degree of management, though. I also realize that I wouldn't appreciate a lot of the duties associated with their employment, such as attending meetings, giving speeches, traveling abroad, participating in charity events, and interacting with governments. My only responsibilities are to support them, develop and strengthen our corporate culture, and make critical capital allocation decisions. Our managers have honored this trust by exerting themselves and performing well. I believe Ronald Reagan was right when he said, "Hard work probably doesn't kill anyone, but why take the chance? " As a result, I've chosen the simple path of doing nothing but watching excellent managers run their shows.

The ability to acknowledge others' accomplishments may be seen as the antidote to envy, but Buffett excels at this and goes beyond merely praising them; he doesn't have to shrink them in order to use them for his own gain; then, he goes above and beyond simply leaving them undamaged; he shields, inspires, and liberates them so that they can be superior to himself.

Confidence

"I'm not brilliant, but I do hang out in a few smart places,"

There is another level to confidence, one that offers a certain amount of inner restraint, and Buffett's confidence has a very defined nature; that confidence is sound; it is a kind of assurance that exists inside the supportive and imaginative realm and that is nearly a balance between arrogant self-assurance and timid helplessness.

In addition, when people are in a respectful and caring relationship with someone in whose eyes they may see their excellent qualities reflected, confidence may grow. They are able to incorporate what others see into who they are. These two aspects of confidence may be very important to Buffett's growth. However, the way another aspect of his confidence has developed in him, though, is interesting.

You develop true confidence in yourself when you have realistic expectations of yourself. Buffett doesn't buy into the oft-repeated adage that anything is possible if you're smart. He contends that you cannot devote the time necessary to developing genuine confidence without restricting yourself.

He avoids the fallacy of conclusion, which holds that he is good at everything while not being, by focusing on his strengths and excelling at them. As a result, he is content and at ease in his good places without being distracted by an unimportant thing. Buffett thrives in his niche and has been there long enough to gain the familiarity and thorough understanding necessary to inspire trust to the point where he can form reliable conclusions on his own.

Love

"We can give the right people and business a good place to live."

Making billions of dollars is more cold and distant than anything that could be explained by a love understanding; therefore, it seems a little odd to include a section on love in a book about Warren Buffett and investing; however, Buffett's relationship with money, and how it overflows into his love for people who make it for him, is the foundation of everything.

How can we interpret this dynamic as a key component of Warren Buffett's investment success, and what does it all mean? Many people now have a better understanding of Buffett's love of money and how it relates to his great talent. Love deepens our sense of self. Love makes us feel good. Love makes us feel good about ourselves. Love makes us feel good about others. Love makes us feel good about ourselves. Love makes us feel good about ourselves.

The affection that Buffett has for these managers and owners is a mature kind that accepts and appreciates their individuality and needs. Buffett's innate tendency to love others fosters an environment in which others feel loved by him because of his appreciation, acknowledgement, and support of them. This ability and way of being cannot be understated, especially for someone whose investment approach necessitates close interaction with owners and managers. He doesn't hold the individuals he cares about to a high standard. His ability to handle disappointments, difficulties, and obstacles while still loving shows how mature he is. Buffett never lets this passion dominate him, though. He has figured out how to maintain his detachment from his attachment. One may assume that the managers who are loyal to him would feel extremely valuable and worthwhile while also feeling free and independent to carry out their duties. Charlie Munger, our vice chairman, and I each have just two jobs, according to Buffett.

This strategy appears simple: if I were in charge of a golf team and Jack Nicklaus or Arnold Palmer agreed to play for me, neither of them would receive a lot of instructions on how to swing from me. My advice to them [his managers] is straightforward: handle your company as though it were the only thing your family will own in ten years.

It would seem that Buffett has a natural way of making the right people feel as valued as they do. We know that the demands of everyday life make it very difficult for us to constantly let those close to us know the extent to which they are fully appreciated. However, despite having more than seventy of these relationships, Buffett seems to do this with ease.

One of Buffett's great gifts is the ability to select the right people to work with and create a respectful place for them to be free and devote themselves to their tasks without interference from him. He says, "My job is to ensure that I don't do anything that kills [my managers'] love of the business." Explaining how he assesses people with whom he decides to go into business with, he says, "I look into their eyes and try to figure out whether they love the money, or if they love the business. If they don't love the business, I can't put [money] into it..." Choosing the right people is vital for Buffett: "Our attitude, however, fits our personalities and the way we want to live our lives. Churchill once said, "You shape your houses and they shape you." We know how we wish to be shaped. Hence, we would rather achieve a return of x while associating with people whom we strongly like and admire than realize 110% of X by exchanging these relationships for uninteresting or unpleasant ones." Choosing the right people also enables Buffett to satisfy his belief in long-term commitments. He makes choices at a deeper level and is committed to maintaining them over time, but he also expects owners to take responsibility for making themselves rich by nurturing that part of their enterprise that they continue to own. "We need 80%. It is important to us that the family members who run the business remain as owners," Buffett says. This kind of relationship is not characterized by manipulation and rapacious control. Instead, it creates a co-operative, mutual connection through which people feel cared for and experience themselves as separate, valued individuals. It allows his business associates to love him in return and work for him with gratitude, joy, and willingness, combining their self-interest with Buffett's own. Buffett explains: "People...find working for Berkshire Hathaway to be almost identical to running their show."

Buffett's capacity to find contentment and a self-affirming sense of his value within, instead of with others is vital to his ability to seek out gifted individuals and celebrate their superior strength while harnessing it for his wealth creation. Being at peace with envy is a crucial element of the way Buffett can be grateful to the people who make him rich and how they can be grateful to him. This is a big part of how they can love one another. The particular intensity of Buffett's relationship with money and the people who make it for him has created a workplace environment that every owner dreams of: people who are devoted to creating wealth for him while feeling completely at home and integrated with the enterprise of making money for him and themselves. He is explicit about this when he says: "It is a real pleasure to work with managers who enjoy coming to work each morning and once there, instinctively, and unerringly think like owners. We are associated with some of the very best."

One cannot overstate the importance of this dynamic as a key component of

Buffett's extraordinary success as an investor. Buffett chooses his people conditionally. He says, "When you have able managers of high character running businesses about which they are passionate, you can have a dozen or more reporting to you and still have time for an afternoon nap.

What is completely fundamental to Buffett, the genius investor, and Buffett, one of the wealthiest men in the world, is his love of money. It's the love of money that gives him a sense of place, groundedness, and purpose. the real question is how can we make sense of Buffett's love. the answer is that he puts a lot of effort into choosing people to love who are specifically going to be making him a lot of money.

It is clearer than any speculation about the origins of Buffett's love for money that somewhere along the line, making money became at-homeness for Buffett and that's what makes him happy. His humorous but revealingly unorthodox lack of appreciation for the significance of the voyages of discovery is indicative of the unique place of money in his mind.

Simplest Investments For Novices

Buy-ins are the simplest investments for new investors. It implies that you will invest in a stock with the expectation that its value will rise rather than fall. Options include trading in short sells and options. These are really difficult because they are not simple. You want to look for stocks whose price increases have a well-established track record. In order to establish whether a company is currently expensive, it is also crucial to pay attention to the news.

However, for the purposes of this piece, we won't talk about the simplest stock investments. If you have the starting money, you could invest in hundreds of businesses, including Google and Apple.

The S&P 500 is one of the simplest investments for new investors and doesn't list hundreds of companies. It is a collection of elite businesses that present you with a wide range of top performers. You can choose an S&P 500 group, invest your money, and watch for long-term effects.

As you learn more about the stock market, the dos and don'ts, and how to select certain stocks based on technical and fundamental analysis, this will help you get started with your investments.

You can also utilize certain stock research techniques to locate suitable, simple investments. One of the strongest technical analysis strategies for newcomers is support and resistance. It offers obvious indicators of a particular pattern that repeats, allowing you to enter and leave the market with minimal financial loss.

We've already talked about the different kinds of things you can invest in. Mutual funds and index funds like the S&P 500 are your best choice if you want to make simple investments. However, you must be knowledgeable with fundamental and technical analysis if you want to invest with an eye on quick returns and take a more active approach.

Principal Analysis

Your investment plan may include other elements besides fundamental analysis. It is based on the economic data that is made available to investors like you and you. For your stock analysis, some economic data points are more crucial than others.

Economic reports on unemployment, market sentiment, interest rates, and national stability.

Information on a company's development, financial health, and opinion of investors.

These two groups are based both on an individual and global level. When you own stocks in firms like Apple and Dell, you are aware that both are regarded as technology companies and offer computers. While Dell rarely releases new goods, Apple frequently does, and this attracts media attention. The majority of investors are focused on the long term when it comes to Apple, but there are instances when investing based on business news in the same industry might make Dell more alluring for a fast investment.

When you perform fundamental analysis, you need to determine if the market as a whole is worthwhile investing in. The demand for stock shares in particular companies may decline if the US economy is not stable. For instance, if unemployment is high nationwide, as it was from 2008 to 2012, you can be sure that no matter what a technological business releases, sales will be lower than expected and stock prices may drop. A strong economy in the nation where a business is located or, on a global level, if people perceive the globe as more stable for these products, you can be sure that demand will be present.

There are things you may discover about a company's information to determine whether it is a wise investment. When taking a stock position, you want the price to increase both at the entry point and the exit point. If the price starts at $100 and goes up to $200, your profit per share is $100. To do this, a corporation must be in a strong position. A big drop in stock prices can be seen if a firm is investing more in research and development than it has available in the event that sales of its new products are unsuccessful.

A company's stock price will frequently rise when it makes a product promise and experiences higher-than-expected sales. It does not always seem to be this easy. The key idea is that you must be aware of business news. Good news typically results in a larger demand for the stock. Additionally, you should observe what the staff members are doing. A trade for a stock is public when it is made. There are often two factors at play when a CEO sells his shares. Either the CEO lacks faith in the business, or shares are being sold to attract new investors. It all comes down to the company's financial soundness and recent news, both of which are open to the public.

You can tell from news reports whether professional investors are interested in a company or whether they believe another one has a better chance of dominating the market. Sometimes the news is based entirely on company news and information, and other times it is about the expert's predictions coming true. Before making an investment in a firm based on the advice of media experts, you must be able to tell the difference. It requires time.

Technical Assessment

Different is technical analysis. It is anchored in the past. You can examine the Google 5-year chart to discover how the stock price responded to various technological, economic, and news events. Stock charts are not predicated on conjecture or speculation. It is not an arbitrary idea, but rather previous responses to the state of the economy and the market.

This does not imply that you can forecast events with greater precision than through fundamental analysis. In contrast to all the day traders present in the market, a large player may have sufficient volume to affect the trend of the market.

Finding an easy pattern that you can trade on safely is the key. It is referred to as resistance and support. In order to use the support and resistance approach, you must look for an upward and downward trend pattern that does not deviate from a specific low or high in the price of stocks.

Consider that throughout the course of a whole week, you glanced at Google, with a daily high of about $500 and a daily low of about $450. If you enter the market at $450 and have a risk management strategy in place to generate a profit of $40 per share, you would sell your shares before the $500 threshold is reached, but you are almost certain to profit by $40 per share. You understand why the stock price is unable to break above an invisible line. Additionally, you are aware that a price floor prevents the price from falling below a set level.

Support and resistance lines are frequently included in the technical analysis area of charting software. The optimal entry and exit points will be shown by the lines that will be created automatically. This pattern alone can be used for trading.

Without getting too technical, you can profit from a breakout trend on an investment in support and resistance if you are in a position with a trailing stop loss. For instance, if your strategy is designed to make $40, but the exit is not triggered when the trend returns to its bottom, you stay in the position. You gain money when the price rises. Your trade will be liquidated once the breakout trend has ended and a new support level has been established. This is because the trailing stop loss is intended to protect your position should the market move against you.

We won't go into great depth on trailing stop losses right now. Just be aware that you can employ risk management orders to preserve your investment and that you can use a breakout in a support and resistance approach to earn more than you anticipated.

The low that the stock price frequently returns to serves as a support. The high stock price serves as the resistance line. You must keep in mind that the support and resistance levels are approximations. It is not a magic figure, but rather an analysis of the optimal entry and exit locations based on the typical reaction of the movement of the stock price.

Low Moving Average

Another investment approach you may use with stock market investing for novices is SMA, or short moving average. The SMA examines a specific time frame, let's say 20 days. The high the stock reached over the 20-day period without crossing the resistance line should be used as the resistance; the amount should then be divided by 20. It provides you with the typical cost. This also applies to the support line. The SMA often refers to the closing price for each day, which is calculated by adding the closing price total and dividing it by 20. However, you need to know the average high the uptrend reaches before it descends to the average low during the downtrend in order to determine your support and resistance levels as well as entry and exit points.

Once you know these levels, you can choose when to buy and sell a stock. Keep in mind that depending on the period you plan to trade, you can obtain the high and low averages. The low and high prices for the day, broken down into hours, are what you need to trade during the day rather than over a longer time frame of days.

A Successful Penny Stock Trader's Psychology

The largest conflict is not in the world of investments, but rather in a trader's thinking. In order to increase the likelihood that a reader will make a profit, it is best to look at the mindset of a good stock trader as well as the greatest qualities and talents they should acquire. It is best to be ready because the war of the mind is a powerful one. All that makes a person human are their mind and emotions. They undoubtedly factor into every choice you make. But if you can, try to keep some emotional components out of a trading game platform that operates on purely rational principles.

Explaining Trading Psychology

We all know this is a lie, despite how much people would love to say they do not become emotionally involved when it comes to investing. Certain emotions do influence the decisions, which may defy reason and result in huge financial losses. Claims that money has no mental impact on you are absolutely unrealistic and untrue because people have gone to war for it, fought for it, and died for it.

It is best to address the trading mentality that can significantly increase your success in addition to conventional tactics. Although greed and fear are the two emotions that frequently affect traders, there are many other complex emotions that can influence your judgment. But before we get into the fundamentals of trading psychology, let's take a closer look at the two guilty feelings that have the biggest influence on your final choices.

Greed is defined as an excessive desire to get wealth, and it can occasionally impair a person's ability to reason. Because their marketing was an effective approach to remove the reasoning to distinguish true from false, it can imply taking unwarranted risks or falling for scams. Taking a chance might occasionally be advantageous but it can also be risky.

Investors that are greedy may also play the game longer than necessary in an effort to maximize their gains. In bull markets, where investors throw caution to the wind and speculation runs amok, you can observe this feature in action. Therefore, while greed might motivate you to strive for a profit, it can also easily go too far, and this is where you will need to have the ability to strike a balance.

The reverse of confidence is fear, which might make an investor withdraw their money too soon when they consider the risks or opportunities. Investors may behave far too irrationally out of fear of significant losses, which could result in panic selling and a significant loss of earnings. Fear is one of the most frequently experienced emotions, but it is typically never a positive one to feel when it comes to trading. Fear frequently results in other emotions like wrath, anxiety, and even despair, all of which are bad for your overall health and trading decisions.

As a result, neither emotion is perfect for anyone. Regret is one feeling that each of these emotions share, though. This problem may lead to rash choices after errors have already been committed, adding insult to injury.

The Value of Understanding Trading Psychology

Learning trading psychology will help you minimize all types of potential judgment errors, particularly those brought on by feelings and reactions. This is advised, particularly for beginners, for whom everything can undoubtedly seem like a rollercoaster. To avoid becoming overwhelmed, it is essential to prepare oneself beforehand. Is it feasible to think like a robot created to have artificial intelligence? No, you should anticipate experiencing many of these emotions, but whether you succeed or fail in the trading market depends on how you manage them. In reality, decisions based on emotions are probably what led to one of the worst losses. Take the extra time and patience to control your emotions in order to prevent excessive risk.

Understanding when to maintain investments despite anxieties and when to sell them requires the capacity to recognize patterns and techniques without being prejudiced toward any one investment. This is referred to as mastering your emotions. It involves controlling your feelings. This prevents the widespread no-holds-barred attitude that many investors have.

When you overstay your welcome in a terrible deal that is happening, use no-hold and hope. It is clinging to the slim chance that better trades will materialize. This is a very common error that could be avoided if only you could control your emotions. This typically entails an investor developing a strategy but then abandoning it in the vain belief that keeping onto the investment will ultimately pay off despite all the clear indications to the contrary. For your total success, it is crucial to learn how to control your emotions in order to prevent this.

Your capacity for risk management will also significantly increase. Since this is the game you must play in the world of the investor, you can substitute logic and facts for emotional considerations as you eliminate the former. When it is much more rational to do so than if you were acting out of greed or fear, you can decide whether to stay or leave. When it is mentioned, it makes a lot of sense, but putting it into practice in real life is far more difficult.

Trading Personality Types

You must first ascertain your personality type with regard to trading. Knowing your attitude toward investments will help you overcome any weaknesses that come with this former personality. Everyone views investing differently. There are two main instances:

There is a rigorous trader first. This character tends to adhere to both rules and patterns they notice. They also frequently adhere closely to plans. Although anyone with a sound strategy can benefit from this, if the plan goes awry, it could easily work against this personality type. They may have a difficult time coping with feelings like greed and fear; greed for holding fast to the plan even though it is impractical in the hope that everything would turn out okay, or fear that adjusting might somehow undermine the entire plan.

The second type of trader is adaptable. This trader is far more flexible and will make modifications to their strategy mid-trade. Although this can also be a commendable trait for a turbulent trade, the trader is at risk of making hasty decisions or deviating from the path and suffering a significant loss. With this personality feature, fear does, however, seem to be more noticeable. Issues can arise from a readiness to modify plans in response to even the smallest adjustment.

Guidelines for Boosting Trading Psychology

What specifically can you do to enhance your trading mindset? You need to put yourself in the ideal frame of mind, more particularly, the mindset that is appropriate for trading. You need to continuously remind yourself that stock values are not personal. They rely only on data, math, and reasoning to function. You must constantly remind yourself that the investors have no emotions and are only interested in the figures. This is not a struggle of terror or greed, but of strategy and rationality. It may sound unusual, but it is absolutely feasible to give trades a personality or a life when you put a lot of time and effort into your study. A trade should be viewed as being quick and straightforward, especially when dealing with penny stocks.

The secret is to be patient. Any astute investor will inform you of this. It's a good idea to be able to delay or stop yourself before making an impulsive choice. This will not only prevent you from falling victim to some of the most prevalent investing frauds, but it will also quickly increase your success. You can take a deep breath and stand back from any emotions that could be overwhelming you at this particular moment with patience. It allows you to clear your mind before making any judgments and gives you enough time to consider your options. Having the patience to wait will help you avoid falling victim to one of the popular investment scams because the most common trick con artists employ frequently is a sense of hurry and impatience.

Education affects your trading psyche in addition to improving your tactics. The better wealthy you are, the more understanding you have about both the psychological and physical challenges of investing. Without being aware of it, how else could you spot investors succumbing to "fear of missing out"? It is comparable to rage in that realizing your anger is the greatest method to control it. The same is true with investments and education. The more you understand, the better you will be able to emotionally handle it. People worry or are terrified of the things they do not know. Undoubtedly, one of the best ways to deal with your emotional responses to trading is to learn as much as you can about it.

Next, get your thoughts ready for both the best and worst case scenarios. As the old adage goes, "Hope for the best and prepare for the worst." You may enjoy success and have a safety net in case you fail if you do it this way. Imagine yourself succeeding in the industry, and this will undoubtedly spur you on to put in more effort. However, give yourself room to contemplate losing so that you can be prepared for the worst and eliminate the unpleasant surprise factor if things don't work out as planned. The shock aspect won't affect you as much if you use this strategy, which is unfortunate to have to recommend. Although it might appear straightforward, few people approach a trade in this way mentally since many people would rather not pay attention to all the potential drawbacks.

Additionally, when you examine the data displayed on the screen, you can become demoralized. You have to keep reminding yourself that this is actual money you are dealing with. This enables you to exercise more prudence, especially if you tend to be a risk-taker, in your decision-making. It goes without saying that you must concentrate on the fact that money is only that—money—if you struggle with anxiety. Take away any emotional ties you might have to it. Learn the practices of profitable traders.

In addition to trade psychology, users can increase their knowledge through studying habits, which are tricks. Remember that everyone has their own preferred techniques of learning, so pick one and stick with it. Do whatever suits you best, whether it's finding a quiet spot in your home or being with others in a cafeteria. VARK stands for visual, auditory, reading, and kinesthetic learning, which refers to learning through sight, sound, reading, touch, or a combination of all of these. To save a lot of time and work, it is best to understand the finest techniques.

The following phase is practice, which can involve learning terminology or developing tactics and testing them out on simulators. As with any other method of producing money, practice makes perfect, and it is unquestionably crucial when beginning an investment strategy. No matter how much you would yearn for a simple way to get money, something worthwhile will not be simple. However, it's not impossible; all you need is some experience, experimentation, and learning. Even better, if you can, identify a trader to copy and study. Observing their tactics and comprehending their choices will undoubtedly assist you develop your own procedures and practices.

Observe the development you've made in your trading over time. Examine what has improved and consider your earlier strategies. Be critical of them and analyze them. The solution? What was unsuccessful? Where can you make changes? Where do you already need to improve? It is best to think about keeping a trading log so that you may learn from your previous blunders. Keeping track of your journey may require more time and work, but it can help you figure out what went wrong and what went right. The 5 Ws and 1 H questions—where, what, why, when, which, and how—should be your main focus. What went wrong? would be an illustration. When did business turn sour? Why did everything go wrong? How can I stop this from happening again? Which trader/news/source was responsible for the abrupt change in the trade's direction? Which areas should I concentrate on to hone my craft?

How to Maintain Focus After Losses

As losses are inevitable for everybody who becomes an active trader, that is perhaps the most important moment to cultivate sound trading psychology. Be aware that you are not instantly eliminated from the game just because you suffer a loss. It depends on how well you handled the setback and how evenly you distributed your losses. But a loss is a loss, and a trader cannot avoid the fact that this will occasionally happen.

However, it is best to avoid being too depressed after suffering a loss. Consider this only a learning curve and, unless you find a serious problem, continue to your current trading strategy. But while emotions can be out of control, it is best to concentrate on something concrete and sensible. Hold onto any plan of action even more tenaciously than before.

Keep an eye on market patterns because they can help you spot potential future losses and enable you to exit early. establish a mental stop order and don't forget to establish stop orders on your trades that automatically execute when the stock you own reaches a certain price. In other words, if you need to, pull over and stop. This doesn't imply you have to quit completely, but if a loss is really significant, it may be preferable to back off than to get paralyzed by fear and suffer much greater losses than you would have otherwise. It's similar to taking a step back and taking a deep breath when you're angry with someone. The ideal strategy for someone who is just starting out in trading is to give oneself permission to breathe after a prolonged period of tension and loss.

Your trip does not, however, end here. Continue to think of yourself as a student. You will always be learning if you trade. The world is constantly changing, whether it be in terms of the newest fashions, technologies, or software applications. As a result, even the world of investing in penny stocks is evolving. It is therefore best to maintain your discipline in this area.

Feelings That Might Derail Day Trading

You should be aware of the most prevalent emotions that could hinder your success if you day trade. It is preferable to deal with them one at a time and be conscious of them before you begin. Your trip will undoubtedly be aided by your efforts to increase your resilience and strength in the face of them. They include: Boredom. Use your free time to learn more about day trading rather than waste it. However, if you do become sidetracked out of boredom, you'll start taking some foolish chances that won't be worthwhile in the long run. Don't accept that risk because it is essentially gambling, and day trading isn't a casino, as we all know. To make learning more enjoyable, learn to prevent boredom by taking breaks, traveling, and even watching YouTube videos. There are some amazing instructors out there who are committed to imparting the trade in a way that doesn't make you want to lie down and take a nap. An excellent resource for this is YouTube. Another excellent strategy to keep yourself motivated and committed to performing the job you need to do is to watch inspirational videos.

I'm depressed. This is a far more significant obstacle you might encounter and one that traders and investors very frequently experience. Everyone finds it difficult to accept defeat, and some people have gone too far in their attempts to cope with these unpleasant feelings. After suffering a significant loss or a number of smaller losses, many traders may even get despondent. So, before engaging in any trade, it is advisable to approach the financial market with much greater information and awareness of the hazards. The ability to anticipate happiness and disappointment can help. Additionally, never start a deal if you are confident you can lose it. It might be time to reevaluate whether you are suited to be a trader if you are unwilling to even entertain the idea of a loss. Don't let yourself be emotionally hampered by a poor trade, even if you need additional time and guidance. Everyone has terrible days, but how they respond to them determines how successful they are. The main distinction between those who succeed and those who fail is this one. It is how they react during difficult times, not how they react during good times.

● Doubt. Even the most seasoned trader may occasionally suffer moments of doubt when odds and numbers change so quickly. It is a good idea to refrain from second-guessing every decision you make. It can assist to alleviate a lot of the skepticism you may encounter if you enter trading with an open mind and are eager to learn without dwelling. Being a close relative of fear, doubt is a hazardous emotion. It is vital to never regret any judgments you have made, even if they were the wrong ones, because doubt may lead you to make bad decisions just as easily as fear does. When you estimated the number of calories in that chocolate bar from a week ago, that is the one time you are ever permitted to doubt yourself. But avoid having doubts before making a trade because they will simply make things worse.

● Fear. This might be the emotion that dominates the market the most, according to some people. Even the term "fear of missing out" (FOMO) is used to describe the tendency to act irrationally and buy something just because the price is going up or down and other people are doing the same thing. Peer pressure and fear go hand in hand, and when it comes to cryptocurrencies—a market that is more volatile than even penny stocks—anxiety tends to be at its height. Another phobia is the one that makes you hesitate before entering a store. This means that despite the possibilities of a deal, you never feel completely satisfied before entering it. As a result, you most likely miss out on a lot of significant business possibilities and gains within the market system.

• Anger. This typically happens when your worries and uncertainties come reality. There is usually nothing you can do about it right now, so this is the moment to step back and take a deep breath. It serves no purpose to worry about things that are now out of your control. The best course of action is to acknowledge your error, perhaps even by writing it down in a trading notebook, and move on. This is much wiser than acting out of rage, which can make all logic and reason irrelevant. In "revenge trading," you attempt to make up for losses by engaging in increasingly riskier trades, as the name suggests. You are also much more likely to lose money on the majority of those trades than you would if you were calm.

• Worry. After a disastrous deal, this usually serves as a recuperation time. The following few trades you make will undoubtedly make you anxious. Remain calm, please! It is preferable to stay calm because if you are anxious, you can exit a trade too soon or fail to develop a sound strategy. If you are apprehensive, think about picking up your trades slowly again until you regain enough faith in your abilities. Because fear is a close relative of anxiety, it frequently coincides with that feeling. It is best to understand how to manage anxiety in all facets of your life if you experience it outside of the trading environment. This will enhance not just your general mental health but also your trade-related abilities and judgment.

These are all really risky feelings. If necessary, you might think about consulting a specialist to help you handle them. Some are simple to modify, while others, like melancholy or rage, can require some assistance. Making informed decisions and being honest with yourself are both essential for success in the world of investing.

One feeling, greed, while potentially harmful to your health, can also help increase the price of your penny stock, but it is undoubtedly negative for trading success. However, your desire to make money may push you past some terrifying dangers that most people won't even think about taking. But for this reason, it is preferable to establish a healthy balance between your desire to work hard and your level of risk aversion. In this manner, you can take chances but exit the game if it does turn out to be a little too risky.

Setting defined goals is crucial for you as a result. To operate investments and trades, there is no black-and-white trading. If there were, trading would undoubtedly be profitable for everyone. Instead, it resembles navigating uncharted waters. It takes time, effort, and experience to learn how to control your emotions.

www.ingramcontent.com/pod-product-compliance
Lightning Source LLC
Chambersburg PA
CBHW071643210326
41597CB00017B/2097